A note on the text:

For this new edition of *The Life of Our Lord*, the text of the first (1934) edition has been checked and corrected against a microfilm of the manuscript, kindly supplied by The Free Library of Philadelphia. As this was a private document, never prepared for publication, minor amendments have been made to Dickens's punctuation and spelling for the ease of the modern reader. The use of capitals has been modernised.

CONTENTS

LIST OF PLATES

FOREWORD

CHARLES DICKENS was born in 1812 and died in 1870, aged fifty eight. He is one of the greatest of all English writers. The stories he wrote, including *Oliver Twist*, *David Copperfield* and *Great Expectations*, are still read today, and are often turned into films and television serials.

One of the secrets of Dickens's popularity, then and now, is the way in which he makes each reader feel as if he is writing especially for them. In fact, he was writing not for one person but for a huge audience. In *The Life of Our Lord*, though, Dickens *is* writing for particular readers: his own children. He never intended to publish it, and it only appeared in print in 1934, sixty four years after his death.

Dickens wrote *The Life of Our Lord* in 1846. He was already the most famous writer of his day. He had published six successful novels, including *Oliver Twist*, and other very popular books such as the story of Scrooge, *A Christmas Carol*. Earlier that year he had for a short time been editor of a new daily newspaper, *The Daily News*; later, he was to start a new novel, *Dombey and Son*. But while writing *The Life of Our Lord* he was living at Lausanne in Switzerland, overlooking Lake Geneva, taking stock of his life and career.

Dickens believed very deeply in the New Testament, calling it "the best book that ever was or will be known in the world". *The Life of Our Lord* is his retelling of that book. It keeps very close to the Gospels, often echoing the very wording of the Authorised Version. In simplifying the story of Jesus Christ for his children, Dickens had to choose which bits of the story to stress, and which to pass over. He believed strongly that Christ's message of understanding, compassion and charity made a foundation for everyday life, not just for Sunday show. Therefore he underplayed the miraculous side of the New Testament story, to emphasise the human aspect. Dickens's Jesus is a great man—someone we might try to be like—rather than a remote divinity.

Because he was condensing four versions of a very complicated story into a single short narrative, Dickens had to simplify the Gospel accounts. He does this very well. Occasionally, he makes mistakes. He says, for instance, that the Jewish Sabbath is observed on Sunday, rather than Saturday; he confuses Herodias, the enemy of John the Baptist, with her daughter Salome. But none of the mistakes detracts from his main purpose, which is to retell the New Testament simply and lucidly, without any preaching or pomposity.

In *The Life of Our Lord* the story of Jesus Christ is retold by a great storyteller, with the tender care of a father speaking to the children he loves.

N.P.

MY DEAR CHILDREN,

I am very anxious that you should know something about the history of Jesus Christ. For everybody ought to know about him. No one ever lived, who was so good, so kind, so gentle, and so sorry for all people who did wrong, or were in any way ill or miserable, as he was. And as he is now in Heaven, where we hope to go, and all to meet each other after we are dead, and there be happy always together, you never can think what a good place Heaven is, without knowing who he was and what he did.

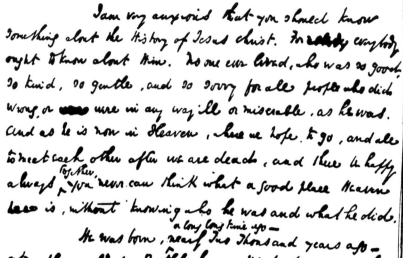

chapter the first.

My Dear Children.

I am very anxious that you should know something about the History of Jesus Christ. For everybody ought to know about Him. No one ever lived, who was so good, so kind, so gentle, and so sorry for all people who did wrong, or were in any way ill or miserable, as he was. And as he is now in Heaven, where we hope to go, and all to meet each other after we are dead, and there be happy always, Together, you never can think what a good place Heaven is, without knowing who he was and what he did.

He was born, a long long time ago — near Two Thousand years ago — at a place called Bethlehem. His father and mother lived in a city called Nazareth, but they were forced by business to travel to Bethlehem. His father's name was Joseph, and his mother's name was Mary. And the town being very full of people, also brought there by business, there was no room for Joseph and Mary in the Inn or in any house; so they went into a Stable to lodge, and in this stable Jesus Christ was born. There was no cradle or anything of that kind there. So

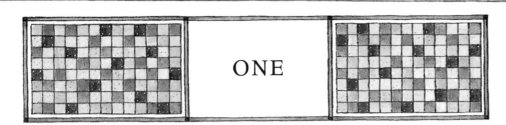

ONE

HE was born a long long time ago—nearly two thousand years ago—at a place called Bethlehem. His father and mother lived in a city called Nazareth, but they were forced by business to travel to Bethlehem. His father's name was Joseph, and his mother's name was Mary. And the town being very full of people, also brought there by business, there was no room for Joseph and Mary in the inn or in any house; so they went into a stable to lodge, and in this stable Jesus Christ was born. There was no cradle or anything of that kind there, so Mary laid her pretty little boy in what is called the manger, which is the place the horses eat out of. And there he fell asleep.

While he was asleep, some shepherds who were watching sheep in the fields, saw an angel from God, all light and beautiful, come moving over the grass towards them. At first they were afraid and fell down and hid their faces. But it said, "There is a child born today in the city of Bethlehem near here, who will grow up to be so good that God will love him as his own son; and he will teach men to love one another, and not to quarrel and hurt one another; and his name will be Jesus Christ; and people will put that name in their prayers, because they will know God loves it, and will know that they should love it too." And then the angel told the shepherds to go to that stable, and look at that little child in the manger. Which they did; and they kneeled down by it in its sleep, and said, "God bless this child!"

Now the great place of all that country was Jerusalem—just as London is the great place in England—and at Jerusalem the king lived, whose name was King Herod. Some wise men came one day, from a country a long way off in the East, and said to the king, "We have seen a star in the sky which teaches us to know that a child is born in Bethlehem who will live to be a man whom all people will love." When King Herod heard this, he was jealous, for he was a wicked man. But he pretended not to be, and said to the wise men, "Whereabouts is this child?" And the wise men said, "We don't know. But we think the star will show us; for the star has been moving on before us, all the way here, and is now standing still in the sky." Then Herod asked them to see if the star would show them where the child lived, and ordered them, if they found the child, to come back to him. So they went out, and the star went on over their heads a little way before them, until it stopped over the house where the child was. This was very wonderful, but God ordered it to be so.

When the star stopped, the wise men went in, and saw the child with Mary his mother. They loved him very much, and gave him some presents. Then they went away. But they did not go back to King Herod; for they thought he was jealous, though he had not said so. So they went away, by night, back into their own country. And an angel came, and told Joseph and Mary to take the child into a country called Egypt, or Herod would kill him. So they escaped too, in the night—the father, the mother and the child—and arrived there, safely.

But when this cruel Herod found that the wise men did not come back to him, and that he could not, therefore, find out where this child, Jesus Christ, lived, he called his soldiers and captains to him, and told them to go and kill all the children in his

dominions that were not more than two years old. The wicked men did so. The mothers of the children ran up and down the streets with them in their arms trying to save them, and hide them in caves and cellars; but it was of no use. The soldiers with their swords killed all the children they could find. This dreadful murder was called the Murder of the Innocents. Because the little children were so innocent.

King Herod hoped that Jesus Christ was one of them. But he was not, as you know, for he had escaped safely into Egypt. And he lived there, with his father and mother, until bad King Herod died.

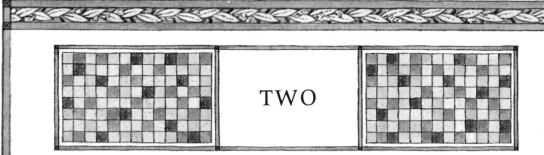

TWO

WHEN King Herod was dead, an angel came to Joseph again, and said he might now go to Jerusalem, and not be afraid for the child's sake. So Joseph and Mary, and her son Jesus Christ (who are commonly called the Holy Family) travelled towards Jerusalem; but hearing on the way that King Herod's son was the new king, and fearing that he, too, might want to hurt the child, they turned out of the way, and went to live in Nazareth. They lived there until Jesus Christ was twelve years old.

Then Joseph and Mary went to Jerusalem to attend a religious feast which used to be held in those days, in the Temple of Jerusalem, which was a great church or cathedral; and they took Jesus Christ with them. And when the feast was over, they travelled away from Jerusalem, back towards their own home in Nazareth, with a great many of their friends and neighbours. For people used, then, to travel a great many together, for fear of robbers; the roads not being so safe and well guarded as they are now, and travelling being much more difficult altogether than it now is.

They travelled on for a whole day, and never knew that Jesus Christ was not with them; for the company being so large, they thought he was somewhere among the people, though they did not see him. But finding that he was not there, and fearing that he was lost, they turned back to Jerusalem in great anxiety to

look for him. They found him, sitting in the Temple, talking about the goodness of God, and how we should all pray to him, with some learned men who were called doctors. They were not what you understand by the word "doctors" now; they did not attend sick people; they were scholars and clever men. And Jesus Christ showed such knowledge in what he said to them, and in the questions he asked them, that they were all astonished.

He went, with Joseph and Mary, home to Nazareth, when they had found him, and lived there until he was thirty or thirty-five years old.

At that time there was a very good man indeed, named John, who was the son of a woman named Elizabeth—the cousin of Mary. And people being wicked, and violent, and killing each other, and not minding their duty towards God, John (to teach them better) went about the country, preaching to them, and entreating them to be better men and women. And because he loved them more than himself, and didn't mind himself when he was doing them good, he was poorly dressed in the skin of a camel, and ate little but some insects called locusts, which he found as he travelled, and wild honey, which the bees left in the hollow trees. You never saw a locust, because they belong to that country near Jerusalem, which is a great way off. So do camels, but I think you have seen a camel? At all events they are brought over here, sometimes; and if you would like to see one, I will show you one.

There was a river, not very far from Jerusalem, called the River Jordan; and in this water, John baptized those people who would come to him, and promise to be better. A great many people went to him in crowds. Jesus Christ went too. But when John saw him, John said, "Why should I baptize you, who are so much better than I!" Jesus Christ made answer, "Suffer it to be so now." So John baptized him. And when he was baptized, the sky opened, and a beautiful bird like a dove came flying down, and the voice of God, speaking up in Heaven, was heard to say, "This is my beloved Son, in whom I am well pleased!"

Jesus Christ then went into a wild and lonely country called the wilderness, and stayed there forty days and forty nights, praying that he might be of use to men and women, and teach them to be better, so that after their deaths, they might be happy in Heaven.

When he came out of the wilderness, he began to cure sick people by only laying his hand upon them; for God had given him power to heal the sick, and to give sight to the blind, and to do many wonderful and solemn things of which I shall tell you more bye and bye, and which are called the miracles of Christ. I wish you would remember that word, because I shall use it again, and I should like you to know that it means something which is very wonderful and which could not be done without God's leave and assistance.

The first miracle which Jesus Christ did was at a place called Cana, where he went to a marriage-feast with Mary his mother. There was no wine; and Mary told him so. There were only six stone water-pots filled with water. But Jesus turned this water into wine, by only lifting up his hand; and all who were there, drank of it.

For God had given Jesus Christ the power to do such wonders; and he did them, that people might know he was not a common man, and might believe what he taught them, and also believe that God had sent him. And many people, hearing this, and hearing that he cured the sick, did begin to believe in him; and great crowds followed him in the streets and on the roads, wherever he went.

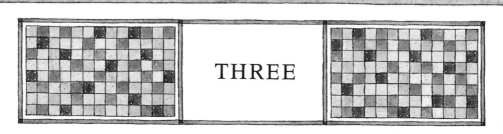

THREE

THAT there might be some good men to go about with him, teaching the people, Jesus Christ chose twelve poor men to be his companions. These twelve are called the apostles or disciples, and he chose them from among poor men, in order that the poor might know—always after that, in all years to come—that Heaven was made for them as well as for the rich, and that God makes no difference between those who wear good clothes and those who go barefoot and in rags. The most miserable, the most ugly, deformed, wretched creatures that live, will be bright angels in Heaven if they are good here on earth. Never forget this, when you are grown up. Never be proud or unkind, my dears, to any poor man, woman or child. If they are bad, think that they would have been better, if they had had kind friends, and good homes, and had been better taught. So, always try to make them better by kind persuading words; and always try to teach them and relieve them if you can. And when people speak ill of the poor and miserable, think how Jesus Christ went among them and taught them, and thought them worthy of his care. And always pity them yourselves, and think as well of them as you can.

The names of the twelve apostles were: Simon Peter, Andrew, James the son of Zebedee, John, Philip, Bartholomew, Thomas, Mathew, James the son of Alphæus, Labbæus, Simon, and Judas Iscariot. This man afterwards betrayed Jesus Christ, as you will

hear bye and bye.

The first four of these were poor fishermen, who were sitting in their boats by the seaside, mending their nets, when Christ passed by. He stopped, and went into Simon Peter's boat, and asked him if he had caught many fish. Peter said no; though they had worked all night with their nets, they had caught nothing. Christ said, "Let down the net again." They did so; and it was immediately so full of fish, that it required the strength of many men (who came and helped them) to lift it out of the water, and even then it was very hard to do. This was another of the miracles of Jesus Christ.

Jesus then said, "Come with me." And they followed him directly. And from that time the twelve disciples or apostles were always with him.

As great crowds of people followed him, and wished to be taught, he went up into a mountain and there preached to them, and gave them, from his own lips, the words of that prayer beginning, "Our Father, which art in Heaven," that you say every night. It is called the Lord's Prayer, because it was first said by Jesus Christ, and because he commanded his disciples to pray in those words.

When he was come down from the mountain, there came to him a man with a dreadful disease called the leprosy. It was common in those times, and those who were ill with it were called lepers. This leper fell at the feet of Jesus Christ, and said, "Lord! If thou wilt, thou cans't make me well!" Jesus, always full of compassion, stretched out his hand, and said, "I will! Be thou well!" And his disease went away, immediately, and he was cured.

Being followed, wherever he went, by great crowds of people,

Jesus went, with his disciples, into a house to rest. While he was sitting inside, some men brought upon a bed a man who was very ill of what is called the palsy, so that he trembled all over from head to foot, and could neither stand nor move. But the crowd being all about the door and windows, and they not being able to get near Jesus Christ, these men climbed up to the roof of the house, which was a low one; and through the tiling at the top, let down the bed, with the sick man upon it, into the room where Jesus sat. When he saw him, Jesus, full of pity, said, "Arise! Take up thy bed, and go to thine own home!" And the man rose up and went away quite well; blessing him, and thanking God.

There was a centurion too, or officer over the soldiers, who came to him, and said, "Lord! My servant lies at home in my house, very ill." Jesus Christ made answer, "I will come and cure him." But the centurion said, "Lord! I am not worthy that thou shoulds't come to my house. Say the word only, and I know he will be cured." Then Jesus Christ, glad that this centurion believed in him so truly, said, "Be it so!" And the servant became well from that moment.

But of all the people who came to him, none were so full of grief and distress as one man who was a ruler or magistrate over many people, and he wrung his hands, and cried, and said, "Oh Lord, my daughter—my beautiful, good, innocent little girl—is dead. Oh come to her, come to her, and lay thy blessed hand upon her, and I know she will revive, and come to life again, and make me and her mother happy. Oh Lord we love her so, we love her so! And she is dead!"

Jesus Christ went out with him, and so did his disciples, and went to his house, where the friends and neighbours were crying

in the room where the poor dead little girl lay, and where there was soft music playing; as there used to be, in those days, when people died. Jesus Christ, looking on her sorrowfully, said—to comfort her poor parents—"She is not dead. She is asleep." Then he commanded the room to be cleared of the people that were in it, and going to the dead child, took her by the hand, and she rose up, quite well, as if she had only been asleep. Oh what a sight it must have been to see her parents clasp her in their arms, and kiss her, and thank God, and Jesus Christ his son, for such great mercy!

But he was always merciful and tender. And because he did such good, and taught people how to love God and how to hope to go to Heaven after death, he was called Our Saviour.

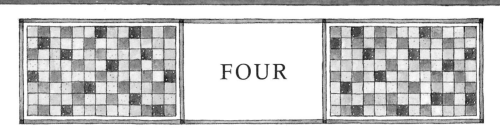

FOUR

THERE were, in that country where Our Saviour performed his miracles, certain people who were called Pharisees. They were very proud, and believed that no people were good but themselves; and they were all afraid of Jesus Christ, because he taught the people better. So were the Jews, in general. Most of the inhabitants of that country were Jews.

Our Saviour, walking once in the fields with his disciples on a Sunday (which the Jews called, and still call, the Sabbath), they gathered some ears of the corn that was growing there to eat. This, the Pharisees said, was wrong; and in the same way, when Our Saviour went into one of their churches—they were called synagogues—and looked compassionately on a poor man who had his hand all withered and wasted away, these Pharisees said, "Is it right to cure people on a Sunday?" Our Saviour answered them by saying, "If any of you had a sheep and it fell into a pit, would you not take it out, even though it happened on a Sunday? And how much better is a man than a sheep!" Then he said to the poor man, "Stretch out thine hand!" And it was cured immediately, and was smooth and useful like the other. So Jesus Christ told them, "You may always do good, no matter what the day is."

There was a city called Nain into which Our Saviour went soon after this, followed by great numbers of people, and especially by those who had sick relations, or friends, or children. For they

brought sick people out into the streets and roads through which he passed, and cried out to him to touch them, and when he did, they became well. Going on, in the midst of this crowd, and near the gate of the city, he met a funeral. It was the funeral of a young man, who was carried on what is called a bier, which was open, as the custom was in that country, and is now in many parts of Italy. His poor mother followed the bier, and wept very much, for she had no other child. When Our Saviour saw her, he was touched to the heart to see her so sorry, and said, "Weep not!" Then, the bearers of the bier standing still, he walked up to it and touched it with his hand, and said, "Young man! Arise." The dead man, coming to life again at the sound of the Saviour's voice, rose up and began to speak. And Jesus Christ leaving him with his mother—ah how happy they both were!—went away.

By this time the crowd was so very great that Jesus Christ went down to the waterside, to go in a boat, to a more retired place. And in the boat he fell asleep, while his disciples were sitting on the deck. While he was still sleeping a violent storm arose, so that the waves washed over the boat, and the howling wind so rocked and shook it, that they thought it would sink. In their fright the disciples awoke Our Saviour, and said, "Lord! Save us, or we are lost!" He stood up, and raising his arm, said to the rolling sea and to the whistling wind, "Peace! Be still!" And immediately it was calm and pleasant weather, and the boat went safely on, through the smooth waters.

When they came to the other side of the water they had to pass a wild and lonely burying-ground that was outside the city to which they were going. All burying-grounds were outside cities in those times. In this place there was a dreadful madman who lived among the tombs, and howled all day and night, so that it

made travellers afraid to hear him. They had tried to chain him, but he broke his chains, he was so strong; and he would throw himself on the sharp stones, and cut himself in the most dreadful manner; crying and howling all the while. When this wretched man saw Jesus Christ a long way off, he cried out, "It is the Son of God! Oh Son of God, do not torment me!" Jesus, coming near him, perceived that he was torn by an evil spirit, and cast the madness out of him, and into a herd of swine (or pigs) who were feeding close by, and who directly ran headlong down a steep place leading into the sea and were dashed to pieces.

Now Herod, the son of that cruel king who murdered the Innocents, reigning over the people there, and hearing that Jesus Christ was doing these wonders, and was giving sight to the blind and causing the deaf to hear, and the dumb to speak, and the lame to walk, and that he was followed by multitudes and multitudes of people—Herod, hearing this, said, "This man is a companion and friend of John the Baptist." John was the good man, you recollect, who wore a garment made of camel's hair, and ate wild honey. Herod had taken him prisoner, because he taught and preached to the people; and had him then locked up in the prisons of his palace.

While Herod was in this angry humour with John, his birthday came; and his daughter, Herodias, who was a fine dancer, danced before him to please him. She pleased him so much that he swore an oath he would give her whatever she would ask him for. "Then," said she, "father, give me the head of John the Baptist in a charger." For she hated John, and was a wicked, cruel woman.

The king was sorry, for though he had John prisoner, he did not wish to kill him; but having sworn that he would give her what she asked for, he sent some soldiers down into the prison, with directions to cut off the head of John the Baptist, and give it to Herodias. This they did, and took it to her, as she had said, in a charger, which was a kind of dish. When Jesus Christ heard from the apostles of this cruel deed, he left that city, and went with them (after they had privately buried John's body in the night) to another place.

FIVE

ONE of the Pharisees begged Our Saviour to go into his house, and eat with him. And while Our Saviour sat eating at the table, there crept into the room a woman of that city who had led a bad and sinful life, and was ashamed that the Son of God should see her; and yet she trusted so much to his goodness, and his compassion for all who, having done wrong, were truly sorry for it in their hearts, that, by little and little, she went behind the seat on which he sat, and dropped down at his feet, and wetted them with her sorrowful tears; then she kissed them and dried them on her long hair, and rubbed them with some sweet-smelling ointment she had brought with her in a box. Her name was Mary Magdalene.

When the Pharisee saw that Jesus permitted this woman to touch him, he said within himself that Jesus did not know how wicked she had been. But Jesus Christ, who knew his thoughts, said to him, "Simon,"—for that was his name—"if a man had debtors, one of whom owed him five hundred pence, and one of whom owed him only fifty pence, and he forgave them both their debts, which of those two debtors do you think would love him most?" Simon answered, "I suppose that one whom he forgave most." Jesus told him he was right, and said, "As God forgives this woman so much sin, she will love him, I hope, the more." And he said to her, "God forgives you!" The company who were present wondered that Jesus Christ had power to

forgive sins, but God had given it to him. And the woman, thanking him for all his mercy, went away.

We learn from this, that we must always forgive those who have done us any harm, when they come to us and say they are truly sorry for it. Even if they do not come and say so, we must still forgive them, and never hate them or be unkind to them, if we would hope that God will forgive us.

After this, there was a great feast of the Jews, and Jesus Christ went to Jerusalem. There was, near the sheep market in that place, a pool, or pond, called Bethesda, having five gates to it; and at the time of the year when that feast took place great numbers of sick people and cripples went to this pool to bathe in it, believing that an angel came and stirred the water, and that whoever went in first after the angel had done so was cured of any illness he or she had, whatever it might be. Among these poor persons was one man who had been ill thirty eight years; and he told Jesus Christ (who took pity on him when he saw him lying on his bed alone, with no one to help him) that he never could be dipped in the pool, because he was so weak and ill that he could not move to get there. Our Saviour said to him, "Take up thy bed and go away." And he went away, quite well.

Many Jews saw this; and when they saw it, they hated Jesus Christ the more; knowing that the people, being taught and cured by him, would not believe their priests, who told the people what was not true, and deceived them. So they said to one another that Jesus Christ should be killed, because he cured people on the Sabbath day (which was against their strict law) and because he called himself the Son of God. And they tried to raise enemies against him, and to get the crowd in the streets to murder him.

But the crowd followed him wherever he went, blessing him, and praying to be taught and cured; for they knew he did nothing but good. Jesus going with his disciples over a sea called the Sea of Tiberias, and sitting with them on a hillside, saw great numbers of these poor people waiting below, and said to the apostle Philip, "Where shall we buy bread, that they may eat and be refreshed, after their long journey?" Philip answered, "Lord, two hundred pennyworth of bread would not be enough for so many people, and we have none." "We have only", said another apostle—Andrew, Simon Peter's brother—"five small barley loaves, and two little fish, belonging to a lad who is among us. What are they, among so many!" Jesus Christ said, "Let them all sit down!" They did; there being a great deal of grass in that place. When they were all seated, Jesus took the bread, and looked up to Heaven, and blessed it, and broke it, and handed it in pieces to the apostles, who handed it to the people. And of those five little loaves, and two fish, five thousand men, besides women and children, ate, and had enough; and when they were all satisfied, there were gathered up twelve baskets full of what was left. This was another of the miracles of Jesus Christ.

Our Saviour then sent his disciples away in a boat, across the water, and said he would follow them presently, when he had dismissed the people. The people being gone, he remained by himself to pray; so that the night came on, and the disciples were still rowing on the water in their boat, wondering when Christ would come. Late in the night, when the wind was against them and the waves were running high, they saw him coming walking towards them on the water, as if it were dry land. When they saw this, they were terrified, and cried out, but Jesus said, "It is I. Be not afraid!" Peter, taking courage, said, "Lord, if it be thou, tell

me to come to thee upon the water." Jesus Christ said, "Come!" Peter then walked towards him, but seeing the angry waves, and hearing the wind roar, he was frightened and began to sink, and would have done so, but that Jesus took him by the hand, and led him into the boat. Then, in a moment, the wind went down; and the disciples said to one another, "It is true! He is the Son of God!"

Jesus did many more miracles after this happened and cured the sick in great numbers; making the lame walk, and the dumb speak, and the blind see. And being again surrounded by a great crowd who were faint and hungry, and had been with him for three days, eating little, he took from his disciples seven loaves and a few fish, and again divided them among the people, who were four thousand in number. They all ate, and had enough; and of what was left, there were gathered up seven baskets full.

He now divided the disciples, and sent them into many towns and villages, teaching the people, and giving them power to cure, in the name of God, all those who were ill. And at this time he began to tell them (for he knew what would happen) that he must one day go back to Jerusalem where he would suffer a great deal, and where he would certainly be put to death. But he said to them that on the third day after he was dead, he would rise from the grave, and ascend to Heaven, where he would sit at the right hand of God, beseeching God's pardon to sinners.

SIX

Six days after the last miracle of the loaves and fish, Jesus Christ went up into a high mountain with only three of the disciples—Peter, James and John. While he was speaking to them there, suddenly his face began to shine as if it were the sun, and the robes he wore, which were white, glistened and shone like sparkling silver, and he stood before them like an angel. A bright cloud overshadowed them at the same time; and a voice, speaking from the cloud, was heard to say, "This is my beloved Son in whom I am well pleased. Hear ye him!" At which the three disciples fell on their knees and covered their faces, being afraid.

This is called the transfiguration of Our Saviour.

When they were come down from this mountain, and were among the people again, a man knelt at the feet of Jesus Christ, and said, "Lord have mercy on my son, for he is mad and cannot help himself, and sometimes falls into the fire, and sometimes into the water, and covers himself with scars and sores. Some of thy disciples have tried to cure him, but could not." Our Saviour cured the child immediately; and turning to his disciples told them they had not been able to cure him themselves, because they did not believe in him so truly as he had hoped.

The disciples asked him, "Master, who is greatest in the kingdom of Heaven?" Jesus called a little child to him, and took him in his arms, and stood him among them, and answered, "A

child like this. I say unto you that none but those who are as humble as little children shall enter into Heaven. Whosoever shall receive one such little child in my name receiveth me. But whosoever hurts one of them, it were better for him that he had a millstone tied about his neck, and were drowned in the depths of the sea. The angels are all children." Our Saviour loved the child, and loved all children. Yes, and all the world. No one ever loved all people so well and so truly as he did.

Peter asked him, "Lord, how often shall I forgive any one who offends me? Seven times?" Our Saviour answered, "Seventy times seven times, and more than that. For how can you hope that God will forgive you, when you do wrong, unless you forgive all other people!"

And he told his disciples this story. He said, there was once a servant who owed his master a great deal of money, and could not pay it, at which the master, being very angry, was going to have this servant sold for a slave. But the servant kneeling down and begging his master's pardon with great sorrow, the master forgave him. Now this same servant had a fellow-servant who owed him a hundred pence, and instead of being kind and forgiving to this poor man, as his master had been to him, he put him in prison for the debt. His master, hearing of it, went to him, and said, "Oh wicked servant, I forgave you. Why did you not forgive your fellow-servant!" And because he had not done so, his master turned him away into great misery. "So," said Our Saviour, "how can you expect God to forgive you, if you do not forgive others!" This is the meaning of that part of the Lord's Prayer, where we say "forgive us our trespasses"—that word means faults—"as we forgive them that trespass against us."

And he told them another story, and said, "There was a certain

farmer once, who had a vineyard, and he went out early in the morning, and agreed with some labourers to work there all day, for a penny. And bye and bye, when it was later, he went out again and engaged some more labourers on the same terms; and bye and bye went out again; and so on, several times, until the afternoon. When the day was over, and they all came to be paid, those who had worked since morning complained that those who had not begun to work until late in the day had the same money as themselves, and they said it was not fair. But the master said, 'Friend, I agreed with you for a penny; and is it less money to you, because I give the same money to another man?' "

Our Saviour meant to teach them by this that people who have done good all their lives long will go to Heaven after they are dead. But that people who have been wicked, because of their being miserable, or not having parents and friends to take care of them when young, and who are truly sorry for it, however late in their lives, and pray God to forgive them, will be forgiven and will go to Heaven too. He taught his disciples in these stories, because he knew the people liked to hear them, and would remember what he said better, if he said it in that way. They are called parables—the parables of Our Saviour; and I wish you to remember that word, as I shall soon have some more of these parables to tell you about.

The people listened to all that Our Saviour said, but were not agreed among themselves about him. The Pharisees and Jews had spoken to some of them against him, and some of them were inclined to do him harm and even to murder him. But they were afraid as yet, to do him any harm, because of his goodness, and his looking so divine and grand—although he was very simply dressed, almost like the poor people—that they could hardly

bear to meet his eyes.

One morning, he was sitting in a place called the Mount of Olives, teaching the people who were all clustered round him, listening and learning attentively, when a great noise was heard, and a crowd of Pharisees, and some other people like them, called scribes, came running in, with great cries and shouts, dragging among them a woman who had done wrong. And they all cried out together, "Master! Look at this woman. The law says she shall be pelted with stones until she is dead. But what say you? What say you?"

Jesus looked upon the noisy crowd attentively, and knew that they had come to make him say the law was wrong and cruel; and that if he said so, they would make it a charge against him and would kill him. They were ashamed and afraid as he looked into their faces, but they still cried out, "Come! What say you master? What say you?"

Jesus stooped down, and wrote with his finger in the sand on the ground, "He that is without sin among you, let him throw the first stone at her." As they read this, looking over one another's shoulders, and as he repeated the words to them, they went away, one by one, ashamed, until not a man of all the noisy crowd was left there; and Jesus Christ, and the woman, hiding her face in her hands, alone remained.

Then said Jesus Christ, "Woman, where are thine accusers? Hath no man condemned thee?" She answered, trembling, "No, Lord!" Then said Our Saviour, "Neither do *I* condemn thee. Go! and sin no more!"

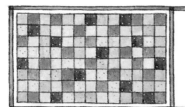

SEVEN

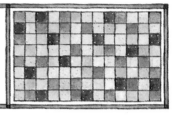

As Our Saviour sat teaching the people and answering their questions, a certain lawyer stood up, and said, "Master, what shall I do, that I may live again in happiness after I am dead?" Jesus said to him, "The first of all the commandments is: the Lord our God is one Lord; and thou shalt love the Lord thy God with all thy heart, and with all thy soul, and with all thy mind, and with all thy strength. And the second is like unto it: thou shalt love thy neighbour as thyself. There is none other commandment greater than these."

Then the lawyer said, "But who *is* my neighbour? Tell me that I may know." Jesus answered in this parable:

"There was once a traveller," he said, "journeying from Jerusalem to Jericho, who fell among thieves; and they robbed him of his clothes and wounded him, and went away, leaving him half dead upon the road. A priest, happening to pass that way, while the poor man lay there, saw him, but took no notice, and passed by, on the other side. Another man, a Levite, came that way, and also saw him; but he only looked at him for a moment, and then passed by, also. But a certain Samaritan who came travelling along that road, no sooner saw him than he had compassion on him, and dressed his wounds with oil and wine, and set him on the beast he rode himself, and took him to an inn, and next morning took out of his pocket two pence and gave them to the landlord, saying, 'Take care of him and whatever you may spend beyond this in doing so, I will repay you when I come here again.' Now which of these three men," said Our Saviour to the lawyer, "do you think should be called the neighbour of him who fell among the thieves?" The lawyer said, "The man who showed compassion on him." "True," replied Our Saviour. "Go thou and do likewise! Be compassionate to all men. For all men are your neighbours and brothers."

And he told them this parable, of which the meaning is, that we are never to be proud, or think ourselves very good, before God, but are always to be humble. He said, "When you are invited to a feast or wedding, do not sit down in the best place, lest some more honoured man should come, and claim that seat. But sit down in the lowest place, and a better will be offered you if you deserve it. For whosoever exalteth himself shall be abased and whosoever humbleth himself shall be exalted."

He also told them this parable. "There was a certain man who prepared a great supper, and invited many people, and sent his servant round to them when supper was ready to tell them they were waited for. Upon this, they made excuses. One said he had bought a piece of ground and must go to look at it. Another that he had bought five yoke of oxen, and must go to try them. Another, that he was newly married, and could not come. When the master of the house heard this, he was angry, and told the servant to go into the streets, and into the highroads, and among the hedges, and invite the poor, the lame, the maimed and the blind to supper instead."

The meaning of Our Saviour in telling them this parable was that those who are too busy with their own profits and pleasures to think of God and of doing good, will not find such favour with him as the sick and miserable.

It happened that Our Saviour, being in the city of Jericho, saw, looking down upon him over the heads of the crowd, from a tree into which he had climbed for that purpose, a man named Zacchæus, who was regarded as a common kind of man, and a sinner, but to whom Jesus Christ called out, as he passed along, that he would come and eat with him in his house that day. Those proud men, the Pharisees and scribes, hearing this, muttered among themselves, and said, "He eats with sinners." In answer to them, Jesus related this parable, which is usually called the parable of the Prodigal Son.

"There was once a man", he told them, "who had two sons; and the younger of them said one day, 'Father, give me my share of your riches now, and let me do with it what I please.' The father granting his request, he travelled away with his money into a distant country, and soon spent it in riotous living.

When he had spent all, there came a time, through all that country, of great public distress and famine, when there was no bread, and when the corn, and the grass, and all the things that grow in the ground, were all dried up and blighted. The Prodigal Son fell into such distress and hunger, that he hired himself out as a servant to feed swine in the fields. And he would have been glad to eat even the poor coarse husks that the swine were fed with, but his master gave him none. In this distress, he said to himself, 'How many of my father's servants have bread enough, and to spare, while I perish with hunger! I will arise and go to my father, and will say unto him, Father! I have sinned against Heaven, and before thee, and am no more worthy to be called thy son!'

And so he travelled back again, in great pain and sorrow and difficulty, to his father's house. When he was yet a great way off, his father saw him, and knew him in the midst of all his rags and misery, and ran towards him, and wept, and fell upon his neck, and kissed him. And he told his servants to clothe this poor repentant son in the best robes, and to make a great feast to celebrate his return. Which was done; and they began to be merry.

But the eldest son, who had been in the field and knew nothing of his brother's return, coming to the house and hearing the music and dancing, called to one of the servants, and asked him what it meant. To this the servant made answer that his brother had come home, and that his father was joyful because of his return. At this, the elder brother was angry and would not go into the house; so the father, hearing of it, came out to persuade him.

'Father,' said the elder brother, 'you do not treat me justly, to show so much joy for my younger brother's return. For these many years I have remained with you constantly, and have been true to you, yet you have never made a feast for me. But when my younger brother returns, who has been prodigal, and riotous, and spent his money in many bad ways, you are full of delight, and the whole house makes merry!' 'Son,' returned the father, 'you have always been with me, and all I have is yours. But we thought your brother dead, and he is alive. He was lost, and he is found; and it is natural and right that we should be merry for his unexpected return to his old home.' "

By this, Our Saviour meant to teach that those who have done wrong and forgotten God are always welcome to him and will always receive his mercy, if they will only return to him in sorrow for the sin of which they have been guilty.

Now the Pharisees received these lessons from Our Saviour

scornfully; for they were rich, and covetous, and thought themselves superior to all mankind. As a warning to them, Christ related this parable of Dives and Lazarus.

"There was a certain rich man who was clothed in purple and fine linen, and fared sumptuously every day. And there was a certain beggar, named Lazarus, who was laid at his gate, full of sores, and desiring to be fed with the crumbs which fell from the rich man's table. Moreover, the dogs came and licked his sores.

And it came to pass that the beggar died, and was carried by the angels into Abraham's bosom—Abraham had been a very good man who lived many years before that time, and was then in Heaven. The rich man also died and was buried. And in Hell, he lifted up his eyes, being in torments, and saw Abraham afar off, and Lazarus. And he cried and said, 'Father Abraham have mercy on me, and send Lazarus that he may dip the tip of his finger in water and cool my tongue, for I am tormented in this flame.' But Abraham said, 'Son, remember that in thy lifetime thou receivedst good things, and likewise Lazarus evil things. But now, he is comforted, and thou art tormented!'"

And among other parables, Christ said to these same Pharisees, because of their pride, that two men once went up into the Temple, to pray; of whom, one was a Pharisee, and one a publican. The Pharisee said, "God I thank thee, that I am not unjust as other men are, or bad as this publican is!" The publican, standing afar off, would not lift up his eyes to Heaven, but struck his breast, and only said, "God be merciful to me, a sinner!" And God—Our Saviour told them—would be merciful to that man rather than the other, and would be better pleased with his prayer, because he made it with a humble and a lowly heart.

The Pharisees were so angry at being taught these things that they employed some spies to ask Our Saviour questions, and try to entrap him into saying something which was against the law. The emperor of that country, who was called Cæsar, having commanded tribute-money to be regularly paid to him by the people, and being cruel against any one who disputed his right to it, these spies thought they might, perhaps, induce Our Saviour to say it was an unjust payment, and so to bring himself under the emperor's displeasure. Therefore, pretending to be very humble, they came to him and said, "Master you teach the word of God rightly, and do not respect persons on account of their wealth or high station. Tell us, is it lawful that we should pay tribute to Cæsar?" Christ, who knew their thoughts, replied, "Why do you ask? Show me a penny." They did so. "Whose image, and whose name, is this upon it?" he asked them. They said, "Cæsar's." "Then," said he, "render unto Cæsar the things that are Cæsar's."

So they left him; very much enraged and disappointed that they could not entrap him. But Our Saviour knew their hearts and thoughts, as well as he knew that other men were conspiring against him, and that he would soon be put to death.

As he was teaching them thus, he sat near the public treasury, where people as they passed along the street were accustomed to drop money into a box for the poor; and many rich persons, passing while Jesus sat there, had put in a great deal of money. At last there came a poor widow who dropped in two mites, each half a farthing in value, and then went quietly away. Jesus, seeing her do this as he rose to leave the place, called his disciples about him, and said to them that that poor widow had been more truly charitable than all the rest who had given money that day; for the others were rich and would never miss what they had given, but she was very poor, and had given those two mites which might have bought her bread to eat.

Let us never forget what the poor widow did, when we think we are charitable.

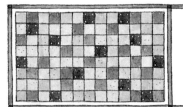

EIGHT

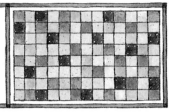

THERE was a certain man named Lazarus of Bethany, who was taken very ill; and as he was the brother of that Mary who had anointed Christ with ointment, and wiped his feet with her hair, she and her sister Martha sent to him in great trouble, saying, Lord, Lazarus whom you love is sick, and like to die.

Jesus did not go to them for two days after receiving this message; but when that time was past, he said to his disciples, "Lazarus is dead. Let us go to Bethany." When they arrived there (it was a place very near to Jerusalem) they found, as Jesus had foretold, that Lazarus was dead, and had been dead and buried four days.

When Martha heard that Jesus was coming, she rose up from among the people who had come to console with her on her poor brother's death, and ran to meet him; leaving her sister Mary weeping, in the house. When Martha saw him, she burst into tears, and said, "Oh Lord if thou hads't been here, my brother would not have died." "Thy brother shall rise again," returned Our Saviour. "I know he will, and I believe he will, Lord, at the Resurrection on the last day," said Martha.

Jesus said to her, "I am the Resurrection and the Life. Dost thou believe this?" She answered, "Yes Lord"; and running back to her sister Mary, told her that Christ was come. Mary hearing this, ran out, followed by all those who had been grieving with her in the house, and coming to the place where he was, fell down at his feet upon the ground and wept; and so did all the rest. Jesus was so full of compassion for their sorrow, that he wept too, as he said, "Where have you laid him?" They said, "Lord, come and see!"

He was buried in a cave; and there was a great stone laid upon it. When they all came to the grave, Jesus ordered the stone to be rolled away, which was done. Then, after casting up his eyes, and thanking God, he said, in a loud and solemn voice, "Lazarus, come forth!" and the dead man, Lazarus, restored to life, came out among the people, and went home with his sisters. At this sight, so awful and affecting, many of the people there believed that Christ was indeed the Son of God, come to instruct and save mankind. But others ran to tell the Pharisees; and from that day the Pharisees resolved among themselves—to prevent more people from believing in him—that Jesus should be killed. And they agreed among themselves—meeting in the Temple for that purpose—that if he came into Jerusalem before the Feast of the Passover, which was then approaching, he should be seized.

It was six days before the Passover when Jesus raised Lazarus from the dead; and, at night, when they all sat at supper together, with Lazarus among them, Mary rose up, and took a pound of ointment (which was very precious and costly, and was called ointment of spikenard) and anointed the feet of Jesus Christ with it, and, once again, wiped them on her hair; and the whole house was filled with the pleasant smell of the ointment. Judas Iscariot, one of the disciples, pretended to be angry at this, and said that the ointment might have been sold for three hundred pence, and the money given to the poor. But he only said so, in reality, because he carried the purse, and was (unknown to the rest, at that time) a thief, and wished to get all the money he could. He now began to plot for betraying Christ into the hands of the chief priests.

The Feast of the Passover now drawing very near, Jesus Christ, with his disciples, moved forward towards Jerusalem. When they were come near to that city, he pointed to a village and told two of his disciples to go there, and they would find an ass, with a colt, tied to a tree, which they were to bring to him. Finding those animals exactly as Jesus had described, they brought them away, and Jesus, riding on the ass, entered Jerusalem. An immense crowd of people collected round him as he went along, and throwing their robes on the ground, and cutting down green branches from the trees, and spreading them in his path, they shouted, and cried, "Hosanna to the Son of David!" (David had been a great king there), "He comes in the name of the Lord! This is Jesus, the prophet of Nazareth!" And when Jesus went into the Temple, and cast out the tables of the money-changers who wrongfully sat there, together with people who sold doves; saying, "My father's house is a house of prayer, but ye have made it a den of thieves!"; and when the people and children cried in the Temple, "This is Jesus the prophet of Nazareth," and would not be silenced; and when the blind and lame came flocking there in crowds, and were healed by his hand—the chief priests and scribes and Pharisees were filled with fear and hatred of him. But Jesus continued to heal the sick, and to do good, and went and lodged at Bethany; a place that was very near the city of Jerusalem, but not within the walls.

One night, at that place, he rose from supper at which he was seated with his disciples, and taking a cloth and a basin of water, washed their feet. Simon Peter, one of the disciples, would have

prevented him from washing his feet; but Our Saviour told him that he did this in order that they, remembering it, might be always kind and gentle to one another, and might know no pride or ill-will among themselves.

Then he became sad, and grieved, and looking round on the disciples said, "There is one here, who will betray me." They cried out, one after another, "Is it I, Lord?—Is it I?" But he only answered, "It is one of the twelve that dippeth with me in the dish." One of the disciples, whom Jesus loved, happened to be leaning on his breast at that moment listening to his words, Simon Peter beckoned to him that he should ask the name of this false man. Jesus answered, "It is he to whom I shall give a sop when I have dipped it in the dish," and when he had dipped it, he gave it to Judas Iscariot, saying, "What thou doest, do quickly." Which the other disciples did not understand, but which Judas knew to mean that Christ had read his bad thoughts.

So Judas, taking the sop, went out immediately. It was night, and he went straight to the chief priests and said, "What will you give me, if I deliver him to you?" They agreed to give him thirty pieces of silver; and for this, he undertook soon to betray into their hands, his Lord and master Jesus Christ.

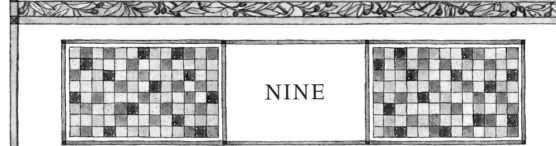

NINE

THE Feast of the Passover being now almost come, Jesus said to two of his disciples, Peter and John, "Go into the city of Jerusalem, and you will meet a man carrying a pitcher of water. Follow him home, and say to him, 'The master says where is the guest-chamber, where he can eat the Passover with his disciples.' And he will show you a large upper room, furnished. There, make ready the supper."

The two disciples found that it happened as Jesus had said; and having met the man with the pitcher of water, and having followed him home, and having been shown the room, they prepared the supper, and Jesus and the other ten apostles came at the usual time, and they all sat down to partake of it together.

It is always called the Last Supper, because this was the last time that Our Saviour ate and drank with his disciples.

And he took bread from the table, and blessed it, and broke it, and gave it to them; and he took the cup of wine, and blessed it, and drank, and gave it to them, saying, "Do this in remembrance of me!" And when they had finished supper, and had sung a hymn, they went out into the Mount of Olives.

There, Jesus told them that he would be seized that night, and that they would all leave him alone and would think only of their own safety. Peter said, earnestly, he never would, for one. "Before the cock crows," returned Our Saviour, "you will deny me thrice." But Peter answered, "No Lord. Though I should die

with thee, I will never deny thee." And all the other disciples said the same.

Jesus then led the way over a brook, called Cedron, into a garden that was called Gethsemane; and walked with three of the disciples into a retired part of the garden. Then he left them as he had left the others, together; saying, "Wait here, and watch!"—and went away and prayed by himself, while they, being weary, fell asleep.

And Christ suffered great sorrow and distress of mind, in his prayers in that garden, because of the wickedness of the men of Jerusalem who were going to kill him; and he shed tears before God, and was in deep and strong affliction.

When his prayers were finished, and he was comforted, he returned to the disciples, and said, "Rise! Let us be going! He is close at hand, who will betray me!"

Now, Judas knew that garden well, for Our Saviour had often walked there, with his disciples; and, almost at the moment when Our Saviour said these words, he came there, accompanied by a strong guard of men and officers, which had been sent by the chief priests and Pharisees. It being dark, they carried lanterns and torches. They were armed with swords and staves too; for they did not know but that the people would rise and defend Jesus Christ; and this made them afraid to seize him boldly in the day, when he sat teaching the people.

As the leader of this guard had never seen Jesus Christ and did not know him from the apostles, Judas had said to them, "The man whom I kiss, will be he." As he advanced to give this wicked kiss, Jesus said to the soldiers, "Whom do you seek?"—"Jesus of Nazareth," they answered. "Then," said Our Saviour, "I am he. Let my disciples here go freely. I am he." Which Judas confirmed,

by saying, "Hail master!" and kissing him. Whereupon Jesus said, "Judas, thou betrayest me with a kiss!"

The guard then ran forward to seize him. No one offered to protect him, except Peter, who, having a sword, drew it, and cut off the right ear of the high priest's servant, who was one of them, and whose name was Malchus. But Jesus made him sheathe his sword, and gave himself up. Then all the disciples forsook him, and fled; and there remained not one—not one—to bear him company.

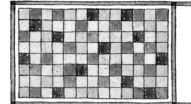 TEN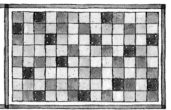

AFTER a short time, Peter and another disciple took heart, and secretly followed the guard to the house of Caiaphas the high priest, whither Jesus was taken, and where the scribes and others were assembled to question him. Peter stood at the door, but the other disciple, who was known to the high priest, went in, and presently returning, asked the woman who kept the door to admit Peter too. She, looking at him, said, "Are you not one of the disciples?" He said, "I am not." So she let him in; and he stood before a fire that was there, warming himself, among the servants and officers who were crowded round it. For it was very cold.

Some of these men asked him the same question as the woman had done, and said, "Are you not one of the disciples?" He again denied it, and said, "I am not." One of them, who was related to that man whose ear Peter had cut off with his sword, said, "Did I not see you in the garden with him?" Peter again denied it with an oath, and said, "I do not know the man." Immediately the cock crew, and Jesus, turning round, looked steadfastly at Peter. Then Peter remembered what he had said—that before the cock crew, he would deny him thrice—and went out, and wept bitterly.

Among other questions that were put to Jesus, the high priest asked him what he had taught the people. To which he answered that he had taught them in the open day, and in the open streets,

and that the priests should ask the people what they had learned of him. One of the officers struck Jesus with his hand for this reply; and two false witnesses coming in, said they had heard him say that he could destroy the Temple of God and build it again in three days. Jesus answered little; but the scribes and priests agreed that he was guilty of blasphemy, and should be put to death; and they spat upon and beat him.

When Judas Iscariot saw that his master was indeed condemned, he was so full of horror for what he had done, that he took the thirty pieces of silver back to the chief priests, and said, "I have betrayed innocent blood! I cannot keep it!" With those words, he threw the money down upon the floor, and rushing away, wild with despair, hanged himself. The rope, being weak, broke with the weight of his body, and it fell down on the ground after death, all bruised and burst—a dreadful sight to see! The chief priests, not knowing what else to do with the thirty pieces of silver, bought a burying-place for strangers with it, the proper name of which was the Potters' Field. But the people called it the Field of Blood ever afterwards.

Jesus was taken from the high priests to the Judgment Hall where Pontius Pilate, the Governor, sat, to administer justice. Pilate (who was not a Jew) said to him, "Your own nation the Jews, and your own priests have delivered you to me. What have you done?" Finding that he had done no harm, Pilate went out and told the Jews so; but they said, "He has been teaching the people what is not true and what is wrong; and he began to do so, long ago, in Galilee." As Herod had the right to punish people who offended against the law in Galilee, Pilate said, "I find no wrong in him. Let him be taken before Herod!"

They carried him accordingly before Herod, where he sat

surrounded by his stern soldiers and men in armour. And these laughed at Jesus, and dressed him, in mockery, in a fine robe, and sent him back to Pilate. And Pilate called the priests and people together again, and said, "I find no wrong in this man; neither does Herod. He has done nothing to deserve death." But they cried out, "He has, he has! Yes, yes! Let him be killed!"

Pilate was troubled in his mind to hear them so clamorous against Jesus Christ. His wife, too, had dreamed all night about it, and sent to him upon the Judgment Seat saying, "Have nothing to do with that just man!" As it was the custom at the Feast of the Passover to give some prisoner his liberty, Pilate endeavoured to persuade the people to ask for the release of Jesus. But they said

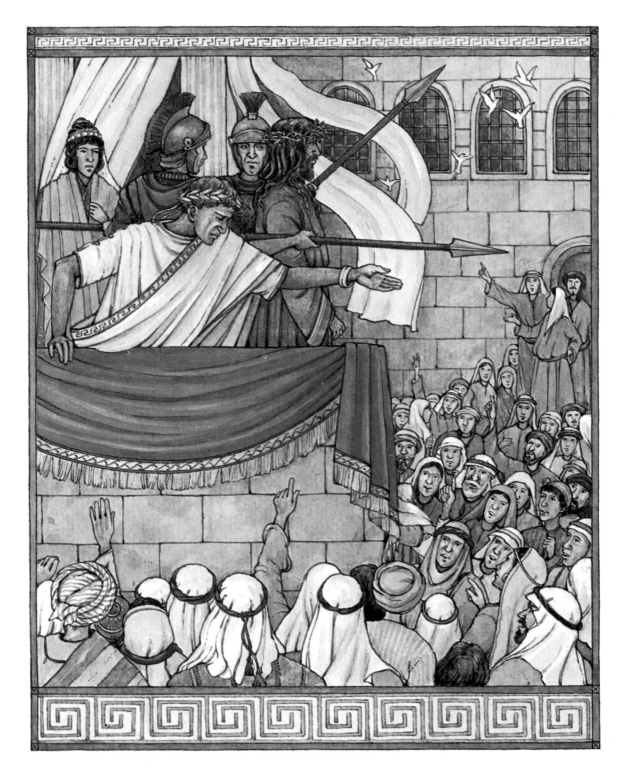

(being very ignorant and passionate, and being told to do so by the priests), "No no, we will not have him released. Release Barabbas, and let this man be crucified!"

Barabbas was a wicked criminal, in jail for his crimes, and in danger of being put to death.

Pilate, finding the people so determined against Jesus, delivered him to the soldiers to be scourged—that is, beaten. They plaited a crown of thorns, and put it on his head, and dressed him in a purple robe, and spat upon him, and struck him with their hands, and said, "Hail, King of the Jews!"—remembering that the crowd had called him the Son of David when he entered into Jerusalem. And they ill-used him in many cruel ways; but Jesus bore it patiently, and only said, "Father! Forgive them! They know not what they do!"

Once more, Pilate brought him out before the people, dressed in the purple robe and crown of thorns, and said, "Behold the man!" They cried out, savagely, "Crucify him! Crucify him!" So did the chief priests and officers. "Take him and crucify him yourselves," said Pilate. "I find no fault in him." But they cried out, "He called himself the Son of God; and that, by the Jewish law, is death! And he called himself King of the Jews; and that is against the Roman law, for we have no king but Cæsar, who is the Roman emperor. If you let him go, you are not Cæsar's friend. Crucify him! Crucify him!"

When Pilate saw that he could not prevail with them, however hard he tried, he called for water, and washing his hands before the crowd, said, "I am innocent of the blood of this just person." Then he delivered him to them to be crucified; and they, shouting and gathering round him, and treating him (who still prayed for them to God) with cruelty and insult, took him away.

ELEVEN

T HAT you may know what the people meant when they said "Crucify him!" I must tell you that in those times, which were very cruel times indeed (let us thank God and Jesus Christ that they are past!) it was the custom to kill people who were sentenced to death by nailing them alive on a great wooden cross, planted upright in the ground, and leaving them there, exposed to the sun and wind, and day and night, until they died of pain and thirst. It was the custom too, to make them walk to the place of execution, carrying the cross-piece of wood to which their hands were to be afterwards nailed; that their shame and suffering might be the greater.

Bearing his cross upon his shoulder, like the commonest and most wicked criminal, Our Blessed Saviour Jesus Christ, surrounded by the persecuting crowd, went out of Jerusalem to a place called in the Hebrew language, Golgotha; that is, the place of a skull. And being come to a hill called Mount Calvary, they hammered cruel nails through his hands and feet and nailed him on the cross, between two other crosses on each of which a common thief was nailed in agony. Over his head, they fastened this writing, "Jesus of Nazareth, the King of the Jews"—in three languages: in Hebrew, in Greek and in Latin.

Meantime, a guard of four soldiers, sitting on the ground, divided his clothes (which they had taken off) into four parcels for themselves, and cast lots for his coat, and sat there, gambling

and talking, while he suffered. They offered him vinegar to drink, mixed with gall; and wine, mixed with myrrh, but he took none. And the wicked people who passed that way mocked him, and said, "If thou be the Son of God, come down from the cross." The chief priests also mocked him, and said, "He came to save sinners. Let him save himself!" One of the thieves too, railed at him, in his torture, and said, "If thou be Christ, save thyself, and us." But the other thief, who was penitent, said, "Lord! Remember me when thou comest into thy kingdom!" And Jesus answered, "Today, thou shalt be with me in paradise."

None were there to take pity on him, but one disciple and four women. God bless those women for their true and tender hearts! They were the mother of Jesus, his mother's sister, Mary the wife of Cleophas, and Mary Magdalene who had twice dried his feet upon her hair. The disciple was he whom Jesus loved—John, who had leaned upon his breast and asked him which was the betrayer. When Jesus saw them standing at the foot of the cross, he said to his mother that John would be her son, to comfort her when he was dead; and from that hour, John was as a son to her, and loved her.

At about the sixth hour, a deep and terrible darkness came over all the land, and lasted until the ninth hour, when Jesus cried out, with a loud voice, "My God, My God, why hast thou forsaken me!" The soldiers, hearing him, dipped a sponge in some vinegar that was standing there, and fastening it to a long reed, put it up to his mouth. When he had received it, he said, "It is finished!"—and crying, "Father! Into thy hands I commend my Spirit!"—died.

Then there was a dreadful earthquake; and the great wall of the Temple cracked; and the rocks were rent asunder. The guard,

terrified at these sights, said to each other, "Surely this was the Son of God!"—and the people who had been watching the cross from a distance (among whom were many women) smote upon their breasts, and went, fearfully and sadly, home.

The next day, being the Sabbath, the Jews were anxious that the bodies should be taken down at once, and made that request to Pilate. Therefore some soldiers came, and broke the legs of the two criminals to kill them; but coming to Jesus, and finding him already dead, they only pierced his side with a spear. From the wound there came out blood and water.

There was a good man named Joseph of Arimathea—a Jewish city—who believed in Christ, and going to Pilate privately (for fear of the Jews) begged that he might have the body. Pilate consenting, he and one Nicodemus rolled it in linen and spices—it was the custom of the Jews to prepare bodies for burial in that way—and buried it in a new tomb or sepulchre, which had been cut out of a rock in a garden near to the place of crucifixion, and where no one had ever yet been buried. They then rolled a great stone to the mouth of the sepulchre, and left Mary Magdalene, and the other Mary, sitting there, watching it.

The chief priests and Pharisees, remembering that Jesus Christ had said to his disciples that he would rise from the grave on the third day after his death, went to Pilate and prayed that the sepulchre might be well taken care of until that day, lest the disciples should steal the body, and afterwards say to the people that Christ was risen from the dead. Pilate agreeing to this, a guard of soldiers was set over it constantly, and the stone was sealed up besides. And so it remained, watched and sealed, until the third day; which was the first day of the week.

When that morning began to dawn, Mary Magdalene and the

other Mary, and some other women, came to the sepulchre, with some more spices which they had prepared. As they were saying to each other, "How shall we roll away the stone?" the earth trembled and shook, and an angel, descending from Heaven, rolled it back, and then sat resting on it. His countenance was like lightning, and his garments were white as snow; and at sight of him, the men of the guard fainted away with fear, as if they were dead.

Mary Magdalene saw the stone rolled away, and waiting to see no more, ran to Peter and John who were coming towards the place, and said, "They have taken away the Lord and we know not where they have laid him!" They immediately ran to the tomb, but John, being the faster of the two, outran the other, and got there first. He stooped down, and looked in, and saw the linen clothes in which the body had been wrapped, lying there; but he did not go in. When Peter came up, he went in, and saw the linen clothes lying in one place, and a napkin that had been bound about the head, in another. John also went in then, and saw the same things. Then they went home, to tell the rest.

But Mary Magdalene remained outside the sepulchre, weeping. After a little time, she stooped down, and looked in, and saw two angels, clothed in white, sitting where the body of Christ had lain. These said to her, "Woman, why weepest thou?" She answered, "Because they have taken away my Lord, and I know not where they have laid him." As she gave this answer, she turned round, and saw Jesus standing behind her, but did not then know him. "Woman," said he, "why weepest thou? What seekest thou?" She, supposing him to be the gardener, replied, "Sir! If thou hast borne my Lord hence, tell me where thou hast laid him, and I will take him away." Jesus pronounced her name,

"Mary." Then she knew him, and, starting, exclaimed, "Master!"—"Touch me not," said Christ; "for I am not yet ascended to my Father; but go to my disciples, and say unto them, I ascend unto my Father, and your Father; and to my God, and to your God!"

Accordingly, Mary Magdalene went and told the disciples that she had seen Christ, and what he had said to her; and with them she found the other women whom she had left at the sepulchre when she had gone to call those two disciples Peter and John. These women told her and the rest that they had seen at the tomb two men in shining garments, at sight of whom they had been afraid, and had bent down, but who had told them that the Lord was risen; and also that as they came to tell this, they had seen Christ on the way, and had held him by the feet, and worshipped him. But these accounts seemed to the apostles at that time as idle tales, and they did not believe them.

The soldiers of the guard too, when they recovered from their fainting-fit, and went to the chief priests to tell them what they had seen, were silenced with large sums of money, and were told by them to say that the disciples had stolen the body away while they were asleep.

But it happened that on that same day, Simon and Cleopas—Simon one of the twelve apostles, and Cleopas one of the followers of Christ—were walking to a village called Emmaus, at some little distance from Jerusalem, and were talking, by the way, upon the death and resurrection of Christ, when they were joined by a stranger, who explained the scriptures to them, and told them a great deal about God, so that they wondered at his knowledge. As the night was fast coming on when they reached the village, they asked this stranger to stay with them, which he

consented to do. When they all three sat down to supper, he took some bread, and blessed it, and broke it, as Christ had done at the Last Supper. Looking on him in wonder they found that his face was changed before them, and that it was Christ himself; and as they looked on him, he disappeared.

They instantly rose up, and returned to Jerusalem, and finding the disciples sitting together, told them what they had seen. While they were speaking, Jesus suddenly stood in the midst of all the company, and said, "Peace be unto ye!" Seeing that they were greatly frightened, he showed them his hands and feet, and invited them to touch him; and, to encourage them and give them time to recover themselves, he ate a piece of broiled fish and a piece of honeycomb before them all.

But Thomas, one of the twelve apostles, was not there at that time; and when the rest said to him afterwards, "We have seen the Lord!" he answered, "Except I shall see in his hands the print of the nails, and thrust my hand into his side, I will not believe!" At that moment, though the doors were all shut, Jesus again appeared, standing among them, and said, "Peace be unto you!" Then he said to Thomas, "Reach hither thy finger, and behold my hands; and reach hither thy hand, and thrust it into my side; and be not faithless, but believing." And Thomas answered, and said to him, "My Lord and my God!" Then said Jesus, "Thomas, because thou hast seen me, thou hast believed. Blessed are they that have not seen me, and yet have believed."

After that time, Jesus Christ was seen by five hundred of his followers at once, and he remained with others of them forty days, teaching them, and instructing them to go forth into the world, and preach his gospel and religion; not minding what wicked men might do to them. And conducting his disciples at

last out of Jerusalem as far as Bethany, he blessed them, and ascended in a cloud to Heaven, and took his place at the right hand of God. And while they gazed into the bright blue sky where he had vanished, two white-robed angels appeared among them, and told them that as they had seen Christ ascend to Heaven, so he would, one day, come descending from it, to judge the world.

WHEN Christ was seen no more, the apostles began to teach the people as he had commanded them. And having chosen a new apostle named Matthias to replace the wicked Judas, they wandered into all countries, telling the people of Christ's life and death—and of his crucifixion and resurrection—and of the lessons he had taught—and baptizing them in Christ's name. And through the power he had given them they healed the sick, and gave sight to the blind, and speech to the dumb, and hearing to the deaf, as he had done. And Peter being thrown into prison was delivered from it, in the dead of night, by an angel; and once, his words before God caused a man named Ananias, and his wife Sapphira, who had told a lie, to be struck down dead upon the earth.

Wherever they went they were persecuted and cruelly treated; and one man named Saul who had held the clothes of some barbarous persons who pelted one of the Christians, named Stephen, to death with stones, was always active in doing them harm. But God turned Saul's heart afterwards; for as he was travelling to Damascus to find out some Christians who were there, and drag them to prison, there shone about him a great light from Heaven; a voice cried, "Saul, Saul, why persecutest thou me!" and he was struck down from his horse, by an invisible hand, in sight of all the guards and soldiers who were riding with him. When they raised him, they found that he was blind; and so he remained for three days, neither eating nor drinking, until one of the Christians (sent to him by an angel for that purpose) restored his sight in the name of Jesus Christ. After which he became a Christian, and preached, and taught, and believed, with the apostles, and did great service.

They took the name of Christians from Our Saviour Christ,

and carried crosses as their sign, because upon a cross he had suffered death. The religions that were then in the world were false and brutal, and encouraged men to violence. Beasts, and even men, were killed in the churches, in the belief that the smell of their blood was pleasant to the gods—there were supposed to be a great many gods—and many most cruel and disgusting ceremonies prevailed. Yet, for all this, and though the Christian religion was such a true, and kind, and good one, the priests of the old religions long persuaded the people to do all possible hurt to the Christians; and Christians were hanged, beheaded, burnt, buried alive, and devoured in theatres by wild beasts for the public amusement, during many years. Nothing would silence them or terrify them though; for they knew that if they did their duty, they would go to Heaven. So thousands upon thousands of Christians sprung up and taught the people and were cruelly killed, and were succeeded by other Christians, until the religion gradually became the great religion of the world.

REMEMBER! It is Christianity *to do good* always—even to those who do evil to us. It is Christianity to love our neighbour as ourself, and to do to all men as we would have them do to us. It is Christianity to be gentle, merciful, and forgiving, and to keep those qualities quiet in our own hearts, and never make a boast of them, or of our prayers or of our love of God, but always to show that we love him by humbly trying to do right in everything. If we do this, and remember the life and lessons of Our Lord Jesus Christ, and try to act up to them, we may confidently hope that God will forgive us our sins and mistakes, and enable us to live and die in peace.

this Parable was, that those who are too busy with their own profits and pleasures, to think of God and of doing good, will not find such favor with him as the sick and miserable.

~~And because~~ It happened that our Saviour, ~~being a~~ being in the city of Jericho, saw, looking down upon him over the heads of the crowd, from a tree into which he had climbed for that purpose, a man named Zacchaeus who was regarded as a common kind of man, and a sinner, but to whom Jesus Christ called out, as He passed along, that He would come and eat with him in his house that day. Those proud men, the Pharisees and the Scribes, hearing this, muttered among themselves, and said "he eats with sinners": In answer to them, Jesus related this Parable, which is usually called <u>The <u>Parable</u> of the <u>Prodigal Son</u></u>.

"There was once a man" he told them, "who had two sons, and the younger of them said one day 'Father, give me my share of your riches now, and let me do with it what I please.' The father granting his request, he travelled away with his money into a distant country, and soon spent it in riotous living.

When he had spent all, there came a time, through all that country, of great public distress and famine, when there was no bread, and the corn, and the grass, and all the things that grow in the ground were all dried up and blighted. The Prodigal Son fell into such distress and hunger, that he hired himself out as a servant to feed swine in the fields. And he would have been glad to eat, even the poor coarse husks that the swine were fed with, but his master gave him none. In this distress, he said to himself 'How many of my drunkeny, until one of the christians (sent by God an angel for that purpose) restored his sight in the name of Jesus christ. after which, he became a christian, and preached, and taught, and believed; with the apostles, and did great service.

They took the name of christians from Our Saviour christ and carried crosses as their sign, because upon a cross He had suffered Death. The religions that were then in the world were false and brutal, and encouraged men to violence. Beasts, and even men, were killed in the churches, under the idea, that the smell of their blood was pleasant to the Gods — there were supposed to be a great many Gods — and many most cruel and disgusting ceremonies prevailed. Yet for all this, and though the christian Religion was such a true, and kind, and good one, the Priests of the old Religions long persuaded the people to do all possible hurt to the christians; and christians were heaped, beheaded, burnt, buried alive, and devoured in Theatres by wild Beasts for the public amusement, during many years. Nothing would silence them, or terrify them though: for they knew that if they did their duty they would go to Heaven. So thousands upon thousands of christians sprung up and taught the people and were cruelly killed and were succeeded by other christians, until the Religion gradually became the great religion of the world.

Remember! It is christianity to do Good always — even to those who do evil to us. It is christianity to love our neighbour as ourself, and to do to all men as we would have them Do to us. It is christianity to be gentle, merciful, and forgiving, and to keep those qualities quiet in our own hearts, and never make a boast of them, or of our prayers, or of our love of God, but always to show that we love Him by humbly trying to do right in everything. If we do this, and remember the life and lessons of Our Lord Jesus christ, and try to act up to them, we may confidently hope that God will forgive us our sins and mistakes, and enable us to live and die in Peace.

THE DICKENS FAMILY PRAYERS

Prayer at Night

O LORD our heavenly Father, almighty and everlasting God, who in thy inestimable goodness hast directed and preserved us during the past day, and brought us to another night surrounded by such great blessings and instances of thy mercy, we beseech thee to hear our heartfelt thanks for all the benefits we enjoy, and our humble prayers that we may cheerfully endeavour every day of our lives to be in some degree more worthy their possession. Sanctify and improve to us any good thought that has been presented to us in any form during this day; forgive us the sins we have committed during its progress and in our past lives; all the wrong we have done; and all the negligences and ignorances of which we have been guilty; and enable us to find in any trials we have undergone or sorrows we have known, or have yet to experience, blessed instructions for our future happiness.

We humbly pray almighty Father for our dear children, that thou wilt vouchsafe to watch over and preserve them from all danger and evil; for ourselves that thou wilt prolong our lives and health and energies and success for many years, for their dear sakes; and for them and us, that thou wilt grant us cheerfulness of spirit—tranquillity and contentment. That we may be honest and true in all our dealings, and gentle and merciful to the faults of others: remembering of how much gentleness and mercy we stand in need ourselves. That we may earnestly try to live in thy true faith, honour and love, and in charity and goodwill with all our fellow creatures. That we may worship thee in every beautiful and wonderful thing thou hast made; and sympathize with the whole world of thy glorious creation. Grant that in the contemplation of thy wisdom and goodness, and in reverence for our Lord Jesus Christ, we may endeavour to do our duty, in those stations of life in which it pleases thee to call us, and be held together in a bond of affection and mutual love which no change or lapse of time can weaken; which shall sustain and teach us to do right in all reverses of good or evil; and which shall comfort and console us most, when we most require support, by filling us, in the hour of sickness and death, with a firm reliance on thee, and the assurance that through thy great mercy we shall meet again in another and happy state of existence beyond the grave, where care and grief and parting are unknown, and where we shall be once again united to the dear friends lost to us on this earth.

Pardon, gracious God, the imperfections of our prayers and thanks, and read them in our hearts rather than in these feeble and imperfect words. Hear our supplications in behalf of the poor, the sick, the destitute and guilty, and for thy blessing on the diffusion of increased happiness, knowledge, and comfort among the great mass of mankind, that they may not be tempted to the commission of crimes which, in want and man's neglect, it is hard to resist. Bless and keep our dear children, and all those who are nearest and dearest to us; and by thy help and our Saviour's teaching, enable us to lay our heads upon our pillows every night, at peace with all the world. And may his grace and thy love and the fellowship of thy Holy Spirit be with us all evermore. Amen.

The Children's Prayer

PRAY GOD who has made everything and is so kind and merciful to everything he has made: pray God to bless my dear Papa and Mama, brothers and sisters, and all my relations and friends: make me a good little child and let me never be naughty and tell a lie, which is a mean and shameful thing. Make me kind to my nurses and servants and to all beggars and poor people and let me never be cruel to any dumb creature, for if I am cruel to anything, even to a poor little fly, you, who are so good, will never love me: and pray God to bless and preserve us all this night and for ever, for the sake of Jesus Christ, our Lord. Amen.

AFTERWORD

IN his novels, Charles Dickens makes merciless fun of religious humbugs. When he himself sounds a religious note, it is often sentimental or commonplace. So he is not generally thought of as a very religious writer, or even as a committed Christian: to some shocked readers of his day, his savage attacks on sham piety and narrow dogmatism made him little better than an atheist. It may seem surprising, then, that he should have taken the time and trouble to write *The Life of Our Lord*. But in his concern for the poor and the powerless, Dickens expresses the essential Christian message more forcefully than many more pious writers.

Dickens's faith is best expressed at the end of his will, made on 12 May 1869. After the formal list of bequests, he writes:

> I commit my soul to the mercy of God through our Lord and Saviour Jesus Christ, and I exhort my dear children humbly to try to guide themselves by the teaching of the New Testament in its broad spirit, and to put no faith in any man's narrow construction of its letter here or there.

This extract from his will testifies, as his friend and biographer John Forster said, to his "unswerving faith in Christianity itself, apart from sects and schisms". Dickens prayed night and morning throughout his life, wrote special prayers for himself, his wife and his children, and in 1846 wrote the "children's New Testament" which is now known as *The Life of Our Lord*.

Dickens had ten children, seven boys and three girls of whom one died in infancy. The eldest, Charles, was born in 1837; the youngest, Edward ("Plorn"), in 1852. He was prompted to write for them a straightforward account of Christ's life and teachings by his intense dislike of religious education which concentrated on doctrinal niceties. He expresses this dislike most clearly in his writings on the so-called Ragged Schools, which were classes organised mainly by churchmen for the scavenger children of the Victorian slums. The well-intentioned teachers laid great store on the catechism; the result, wrote Dickens, was "to perplex the minds of these unfortunate creatures with religious mysteries". He makes fun of this in his account of a Ragged School in *Our Mutual Friend*, where he depicts a teacher "drawling on to My Dearerr Childerrenerr . . . about the beautiful coming to the Sepulchre; and repeating the word Sepulchre (commonly used among infants) five hundred times, and never once hinting what it meant".

Dickens was content to leave the Old Testament as a battlefield for warring sects. When his children left home, he gave each of them a New Testament, not a Bible. It is worth quoting at length the letter he wrote on 26 September 1868 to Plorn, who was emigrating to Australia at the age of sixteen:

> I put a New Testament among your books, for the very same reasons, and with the very same hopes that made me write an easy account of it for you, when you were a little child; because it is the best book that ever was or will be known in the world, and because it teaches you the best lessons by which any human creature who tries to be truthful and faithful to duty can possibly be guided. As your brothers have gone away, one by one, I have written to each such words as I am now writing to you, and have entreated them all to guide themselves by this book, putting aside the interpretations and inventions of Man.
>
> You will remember that you have never at home been harassed about religious observances or mere formalities. I have always been anxious not to weary my children with such things before they are old enough to form opinions respecting them. You will therefore understand the better that I now most solemnly impress upon you the truth and beauty of the Christian religion, as it came from Christ Himself, and the impossibility of your going far wrong if you humbly but heartily respect it.
>
> Only one thing more on this head. The more we are in earnest as to feeling it, the less we are disposed to hold forth about it. Never abandon the wholesome practice of saying your own private prayers, night and morning. I have never abandoned it myself, and I know the comfort of it.

Plorn also took with him a copy of *The Life of Our Lord*, made for him by his sister Mamie. Other copies were made for members of the family, and one for the children of Dickens's friend Mark Lemon, the editor of *Punch*, but it remained always a private family document. Towards the end of his life Dickens was asked by his sister-in-law Georgina Hogarth to consider having it printed; he took a couple of weeks to decide emphatically against publication, a decision which held until 1934, after the death of his last surviving son, Henry.

The first edition of 1934 was transcribed from a manuscript

bequeathed by Henry, which was kept in a case marked with an incorrect date of composition, 1849; Mark Lemon's copy bore the correct date of 1846, which is confirmed from Dickens's letters. This edition has been checked and corrected against the same manuscript. It is written in a bold unhesitating hand with very little major alteration or rewriting, unlike the heavily scored and revised manuscripts of Dickens's fiction. Where a phrase or sentence is deleted or inserted, the changes are clearly contemporary with the main text, rather than afterthoughts. It may be that this was not the first draft, but Dickens seems to have known clearly what he wanted to say and how he wanted to say it. The text is divided into eleven chapters, with a single break in chapter eleven, marked in this edition by a dropped capital. His divisions have been followed here, save that his very personal introductory and closing paragraphs have been separated from the main text.

No doubt if he had consented to publication, Dickens would have tidied up this text, and removed those passages in which he directly addresses his own children. We can be grateful that he did not, for these passages have a charm, immediacy and sense of purpose which makes this a special book: domestic, unpretentious, informal, yet charged with deep feeling.

The uncluttered, lucid narrative is based largely on the Gospels of Luke and John, with elements of Matthew and Mark, and, at the end, the Acts. Dickens was, in the 1840s, drawn to the Unitarian Church, "a religion which has sympathy for men of all creeds and ventures to pass judgement on none". He attended the Unitarian Chapel at Little Portland Street, whose minister Edward Tagart became a personal friend. But his sympathies were essentially Broad Church, and from 1847 onwards he attended the Anglican church near his home at Gad's Hill. He has no theological axe to grind.

Dickens's impatience with "religious mysteries" pervades this abstract of the Gospels. Christ is presented as a man and a great spiritual teacher; the emphasis is on his goodness rather than his divinity. It is true that Dickens nowhere mentions that Jesus Christ was a carpenter, and was deeply, almost hysterically upset when in 1850 the painter Millais exhibited a picture, "The Carpenter's Shop", which seemed to him to display an offensive and irreverent realism. But the miraculous is played down, and the social message of the Gospels is stressed. Matters such as the meaning of communion, the trinity and the virgin birth are glossed over or ignored. Christ does not say "This is my body . . . this is my blood" at the Last Supper; Joseph is referred to as his father, and we are told that Jesus "will grow up to be so good that God will love him as his own son". Because of this emphasis on Christ's humanity, it has seemed right to regularise pronouns referring to him in the lower case: "him" not "Him". Dickens follows no consistent plan in this—or in his capitalisation in general—though as the story nears its climax he becomes more likely to use the reverential capital.

This lack of concern for what some might consider the higher message of salvation does not imply that Dickens did not think deeply about the meaning of religion. He records that when the spirit of Mary Hogarth appeared to him in a dream in 1844, he asked it "in an agony of entreaty", "What is the True religion?" The very last page of his unfinished *Mystery of Edwin Drood* contains a promise of "the Resurrection and the Life". This was written on his last day of consciousness, 8 June 1870, a day on which *The Life of Our Lord* was also on his mind. He had received a letter from a reader complaining about supposed irreverence in the adaptation of a phrase from scripture in chapter 10 of *Edwin Drood*. He wrote:

> I have always striven in my writings to express veneration for the life and lessons of Our Saviour; because I feel it; and because I re-wrote that history for my children—every one of whom knew it from having it repeated to them—long before they could read, and almost as soon as they could speak.
> But I have never made proclamation of this from the house tops.

To proclaim belief from the house tops is, for Dickens, a mark of the humbug. In his preface to the 1847 edition of his first novel, *Pickwick Papers*, he is careful to differentiate between "religion and the cant of religion"; it is this cant which he attacks in his fiction in figures such as the sanctimonious, hypocritical Chadband in *Bleak House*. Even more distressing to Dickens was the use of religion as a form of mental and emotional blackmail or bullying, exemplified by Murdstone in *David Copperfield*, and the sterile Clennam household in *Little Dorrit*. He regarded the rarified academic theology of his day, with its schisms and counter-schisms, "Gorham controversies, and Pusey controversies, and Newman controversies, and twenty other controversies", as mere arid pedantry, irrelevant to the needs of the poor and the suffering who, in religious matters as in social and political questions, remained at the forefront of his consciousness.

Christianity, concludes Dickens, means "to do good". The story of Christ's life is an example of this "good" in action:

> And when people speak ill of the poor and miserable, think how Jesus Christ went among them and taught them, and thought them worthy of his care.

The Life of Our Lord does not read, nor would it be suitable for it to read, like a piece of extravagant Dickensian fiction. It often keeps close to the very wording of the Authorised Version. Nevertheless, it does bear the imprint of his personality, especially in its emphasis on the social application of Christ's teaching, and in its tenderness towards children. In his description of Christ bringing the dead girl back to life in chapter 3, his sympathies, and ours, are brought keenly into play. Again in chapter 6, when the disciples ask, "Who is greatest in the kingdom of Heaven?":

> Jesus called a little child to him, and took him in his arms, and stood him among them, and answered, "A child like this. I say unto you that none but those who are as humble as little children shall enter into Heaven. Whosoever shall receive one such little child in my name receiveth me. But whosoever hurts one of them, it were better for him that he had a millstone tied about his neck, and were drowned in the depths of the sea. The angels are all children."

This part of Christ's teaching is emphasised in accord with Dickens's own rejection of the concept of original sin, and the practice of putting "the fear of God" into little children. As he wrote to a Mrs Godfrey in 1839 about her children's stories:

> I do most decidedly object, and have a most invincible and profound repugnance to that frequent reference to the Almighty in small matters, which so many excellent persons consider necessary in the education of children. I think it monstrous to hold the source of inconceivable mercy and goodness perpetually up to them as an avenging and wrathful God who—making them in His wisdom children before they are men and women—is to punish them awfully for every little venial offence which is almost a necessary part of that stage of life.

Quite rightly, Dickens did not, in making a simple paraphrase of the Gospels suited to the understanding of children, seek to impress his own literary style on the material. He offers a shared reading of the Gospel story, rather than an imaginative recreation of it. Nevertheless, there are resonances with Dickens's other work, most notably with the series of Christmas books he wrote in the 1840s: *A Christmas Carol, The Chimes, The Cricket on the Hearth, The Battle of Life* and *The Haunted Man*. Dickens announced his completion of "the children's New Testament" in a letter to John Forster of 28 June 1846. He then set to work at *Dombey and Son*, breaking off to write *The Battle of Life*. It is worth comparing his description of the transfiguration in *The Life of Our Lord*:

> suddenly his face began to shine as if it were the sun, and the robes he wore, which were white, glistened and shone like sparkling silver, and he stood before them like an angel

with the similar description of Marion at the climax of *The Battle of Life*:

> so beautiful, so happy, so unalloyed by care and trial, so elevated and exalted in her loveliness, that as the setting sun shone brightly on her upturned face, she might have been a spirit visiting the earth upon some healing mission.

No one would claim *The Life of Our Lord* as great literature, but it has been unduly neglected. The transparency of its style, which George Bernard Shaw derided as a "belittling" of the Gospels, is not achieved without a good deal of thought and care. *The Life of Our Lord* is simple, but it is not simplistic.

There are, perhaps inevitably, some areas in which Dickens's wish to be clear leads instead to confusion. It may be deliberate, for instance, that he merges the figures of Herodias and her daughter Salome; it may be a simple mistake. It is certainly an error for him to state, as he does, that the Jewish Sabbath is on Sunday rather than Saturday. More worrying is what Robert Graves called "his total disconnection of Jesus from the Jewish race and religion". In chapter 4, when Dickens writes that "most of the inhabitants of that country were Jews", he fails to mention that Jesus Christ himself was a Jew, and thus lays himself open in the passages on the trial and crucifixion to a charge of anti-semitism. While "the Jews" are undoubtedly portrayed as hostile in *The Life of Our Lord*, this is confined to dramatic set-pieces rather than operating as a pervasive condemnation of race or religion, and certainly was not intended either to instigate or to fuel anti-semitic feeling. Dickens regretted incorporating in the character of Fagin, in

Oliver Twist, so much of the villainous Jew of popular prejudice, and made revisions of the text to modify this. The good Jew Riah in *Our Mutual Friend* was introduced as a deliberate act of atonement.

In essence, *The Life of Our Lord* is a series of vivid dramatic vignettes, arranged almost like scenes shown in a child's coloured toy theatre. It is a technique adapted in a feat of brilliant compression in Dickens's semi-autobiographical essay "The Christmas Tree" in the 1850 Christmas number of his weekly journal *Household Words*:

> But hark! The waits are playing, and they break my childish sleep! What images do I associate with the Christmas music as I see them set forth on the Christmas tree? Known before all the others, keeping far apart from all the others, they gather round my little bed. An angel, speaking to a group of shepherds in a field; some travellers, with eyes uplifted, following a star; a baby in a manger; a child in a spacious temple, talking with grave men; a solemn figure, with a mild and beautiful face, raising a dead girl by the hand; again, near a city gate, calling back the son of a widow, on his bier, to life; a crowd of people looking through the opened roof of a chamber where he sits, and letting down a sick person on a bed, with ropes; the same, in a tempest, walking on the water to a ship; again, on a sea-shore, teaching a great multitude; again, with a child upon his knee, and other children round; again, restoring sight to the blind, speech to the dumb, hearing to the deaf, health to the sick, strength to the lame, knowledge to the ignorant; again, dying upon a cross, watched by armed soldiers, a thick darkness coming on, the earth beginning to shake, and only one voice heard, "Forgive them, for they know not what they do."

These were the images Dickens wished to summon up for his own children in *The Life of Our Lord*: potent, life-affirming images playing out a great story on the stage of a great writer's mind.

NEIL PHILIP
Oxford, 1987